1966 Cowboys

UNITED · STATES · POSTAL · SERVICE

# *1992 Commemorative Stamp Collection*

# Table of Contents

4    Introduction

6    Hummingbirds

8    W.E.B. Du Bois

9    Love

10    Dr. Theodore von Kármán

12    World War II

14    Alaska Highway

15    Dorothy Parker

16    First Voyages of Columbus

18    Winter Olympics

20    World Columbian Stamp Expo '92

21    Juan Rodríguez Cabrillo

22    Summer Olympics

24    Olympic Baseball

25    Minerals

26    Wildflowers

28    Space

30    Kentucky Statehood

31    New York Stock Exchange

32    Wild Animals

34    Christmas

36    Credits

*Their brilliant plumage mirrored on Galapagos Islands waters, flamingos search for small mollusks, crustaceans, algae and diatoms. Facing page: An American astronaut leaves the space shuttle "Discovery" in 1985 to capture, repair, and release a Syncom satellite.*

*"Magic" Johnson dribbles the basketball at one of theUSA's "dream team" victories during Summer Olympic Games in Barcelona. At right, a truck winds through the Cossier Mountains on the Alaska Highway in Yukon, Canada.*

*This collection contains all stamps issued through November 1992.*

Call it a banner year, vintage year, historic or blockbuster year, the U.S. Postal Service in 1992 issued some of the most exciting and varied stamps in decades.

Picking favorites would be up to individuals. The reissue of the philatelically famed Columbian Issue commemoratives, originally issued in 1893, was an eagerly anticipated event for collectors. Reproduced from the original engravings, the 16 stamps were elegantly paired on five souvenir sheets with related steel engravings.

The first U.S. stamps issued in January 1992 were the Winter Olympics stamps, a strip of five in sheet format, which heralded the upcoming Winter Games in Albertville, France. They pictured in stylized, brightly colored renderings speed skating, skiing, ice hockey, bobsled competition and figure skating.

Also in January, the Columbian "Stamp-on-Stamp" was issued, a reproduction of the 1869 stamp that showed Columbus claiming the New World for Spain. It was an appropriate send-off for the rest of the Columbian stamps that followed.

William E.B. Du Bois, brilliant scholar, historian, teacher and activist, became the 15th American to be honored in the Black Heritage Series. Du Bois was an acquaintance of writer, poet and critic Dorothy Parker, whose stamp appeared in August in the Literary Arts Series. Both Du Bois and Parker crusaded vigorously for equality for blacks.

In time for Valentine's Day, springtime wedding invitations and Mother's Day, February brought the popular Love stamp featuring a large red heart and an envelope.

In early April, when winter expired and baseball season began, a stamp celebrated the inclusion of baseball as a medal sport in the 1992 Summer Olympic Games in Barcelona.

Later that month, the United States and Italy jointly issued a block of four Columbian stamps, depicting the four stages of Columbus's saga: seeking Queen Isabella's support for the voyage; his three sailing ships; the sighting of land by Columbus's crew; and the landing in the New World.

May brought the anniversary of the founding of the New York Stock Exchange, which began as an agreement in 1792 among 24 businessmen to establish regulations for an exchange to fill the need occasioned by the colonies' break with England, and became an institution 100 years later.

Also in May a stunning block of four space stamps appeared, jointly issued by the U.S. Postal Service and the Russian postal administration. The block celebrated exploration achievements of the two global powers and looked to a future joint mission to Mars.

May 30 commemorated the 50th anniversary of completion of the Alaska Highway, a critically important overland link between the United States and what was then the Alaska Territory.

June brought the most varied subjects of the year. The first was the Kentucky Statehood commemorative celebrating Kentucky's acceptance as the 15th State in the Union 200 years ago.

Following that issue, Summer Olympics sports of boxing, volleyball, gymnastics, soccer and swimming were depicted on a strip of five stamps. Like the Winter Olympics stamps and the Olympic baseball stamp, these stamps carried the Olympic five-ring logo signifying that the U.S. Postal Service is an official sponsor of the 1992 Olympic Games.

A booklet of hummingbird stamps was issued in mid-June, the peak time of the birds' presence throughout the nation. An example of serendipity in the stamp program: the five brilliantly colored "hummers,' which are indigenous to the United States, would not be here were it not for the glorious wildflowers appearing on the sheet of 50 stamps issued later in July. The flowers' nectar and small insects keep the tiny birds flying and contributing to pollination of more flowers.

In August, the Postal Service issued the second of its mini sheets of 10 stamps commemorating major events of World War II in 1942. Also in August, Dorothy Parker's addition to the Literary Arts Series was warmly received by readers who still quote some of her memorable poems written in the 1920s, 1930s and 1940s.

In August, Dr. Theodore von Kármán, popularly known in scientific and engineering circles as the "father of jet propulsion," received due honors. Von Kármán's theories and experiments

*U.S. Navy (SBD-3) dive bombers destroyed a major part of Japan's fleet in the Battle of Midway in June, 1942. Below: a male Ruby-throated hummingbird plunges his bill in a Trumpet Creeper in search of nectar.*

in rocketry contributed greatly to achievements shown on the four space stamps jointly issued by the U.S. and Russia.

September brought the second in the Mineral Heritage Series with the issuance of four beautiful stamps: copper, wulfenite, azurite and variscite—all found in the United States.

Juan Rodriguez Cabrillo was honored on the 450th anniversary of his landing in 1542 on the west coast of the present United States. The stamp was issued in September at Point Loma National Park, overlooking San Diego Bay in California.

Sure to be a children's favorite, a booklet of five wild animal stamps was issued in October. Of the five species, two threatened with extinction within the next century are the giant panda and the tiger. Also in the booklet are flamingos, king penguins and giraffes.

Closing out the excellent year, the Postal Service issued a block of four antique toy stamps and its traditional stamp featuring a Madonna and Child, attributed to Renaissance artist Giovanni Bellini. Both holiday issues appeared in sheet and booklet form.

A final coincidence: Christopher Columbus and Giovanni Bellini were Italian Renaissance men. Columbus, born in Genoa around 1451, died in 1506; Bellini, born in Venice around 1430, died in 1516.

# Hummingbirds

Hummingbirds, nature's tiniest representatives of the bird family, can fly swiftly or slowly, up, down, sideways, backward or forward. They can hover in place like miniature helicopters, wings whirring at 50 to 80 beats per second.

The five hummingbirds in 1992's commemorative booklet are indigenous to various parts of the United States. As winter nears they migrate to the tropics, where flowers and insects are plentiful. Generally, migratory birds fly north in the spring to nest, and then south in the fall. But one of these birds has a different schedule. The Rufous flies northwest in late winter and southeast in summer, following different routes for each journey. Found as far north as southern Alaska, the Rufous takes advantage of seasonal flowers and is assured of a supply of food during both flights.

The Calliope, with a shorter bill, is the smallest of these five birds. It weighs about one-tenth of an ounce, has a wingspread of about one and one-half inches and can grow to three-and-one-half inches in length. It breeds throughout the west, except for the Pacific coast and the southwest, and can live at an altitude of 10,000 feet, along mountain slopes.

The Ruby-throated "hummer" is the only one that lives throughout the eastern half of the United States and most of southern Canada. Those from the central part of the country migrate south directly through Texas; those in the eastern part of the United States fly non-stop across the Gulf of Mexico to their winter quarters.

The Broad-billed hummingbird nests in arid areas at the base of canyons or along small streambeds in southeastern Arizona, southwestern New Mexico and western Texas.

The Costa's prefers dry climates and environments. Some Costa's are year-round residents in southern California and southwestern Arizona.

Although these mighty midgets have legs, they cannot walk or climb. This doesn't affect their ability to hover while they suck flower nectar through long, slender bills, or capture insects whose protein is essential to maintain their weight. Because they burn energy so rapidly, hummingbirds eat almost constantly to stay alive.

For most birds, the downstroke of wings powers flight, with the upstroke functioning for recovery. The hummingbird "sculls" the air rather than strokes it, thus gaining constant lift with forward-and-backward movement, instead of a flapping up-and-down motion. Their pectoral muscles are larger for their size than any other bird's.

Hummingbirds have been clocked in a wind tunnel at a speed of 27 miles per hour. For long flights they store enough fat in advance to increase their weight by 50 per cent.

Despite their diminutive size, hummingbirds are fearless and aggressive. They attack hawks or crows with swift, darting maneuvers and stabbing beaks and fight with bees for entry rights to nectar-producing flowers.

Although few feathers cover their tough skins, refraction and diffusion of sunlight through the ones they have creates brilliant colors. Famed ornithologist John James Audubon called hummingbirds "glittering fragments of the rainbow."

The hummingbird stamps, in which the birds are pictured with related flora, were designed by Chuck Ripper of Huntington, West Virginia, and were issued on June 15, 1992 in Washington, D.C.

*A Broad-billed hummingbird, wings spread, lights on a twig in Madera Canyon, Arizona. On facing page, clockwise, a young Rufous feeds from a Scarlet Penstemon; a Ruby-throated "hummer" perches on a twig; a female Costa's backs out from an Ocotillo; a tiny Calliope sits on a branch in Mount Pinos, California*

*One of the nation's foremost wildlife illustrators, Chuck Ripper of Huntington, WV is also among this country's most prolific stamp designers. The five 1992 Hummingbird stamps bring his total to 77 designs, including the popular Wildlife pane, FishingFlies, Wildlife Habitats and Coral Reef blocks.*

# W. E. B. Du Bois

William Edward Burghardt Du Bois, of mixed French, Dutch and African parentage, was a controversial and brilliant scholar, author and educator who used his many gifts in a lifelong crusade to promote equal treatment for blacks in a white-dominated world.

Born in Great Barrington, Massachusetts, a great-grandson of a black slave emancipated for his service in the Revolution, Du Bois spent his early childhood at his grandfather's farm. His father, a barber, deserted his family. Will and his mother moved to town, where she worked as a domestic so he could get a good education. He fulfilled her aspirations: the only black in his high school, he won top scholarship honors.

Not until he attended Fisk University, a black school in Nashville, Tennessee, did he experience racial prejudice and separation. After graduating from Fisk in 1888, he studied at Harvard and received a bachelor's degree in Philosophy in 1890. He remained there two more years, studying history and political economy.

Du Bois then studied sociology at the University of Berlin for two years, returned to the United States, taught at Wilberforce University, completed his dissertation and became the first black to receive a doctorate from Harvard.

He taught Latin, Greek, German, English, sociology and history at the Universities of Pennsylvania and Atlanta (now Clark Atlanta), and in 1905 he founded the Niagara Movement, a precursor to the National Association for the Advancement of Colored People, which he co-founded.

Preferring to emulate the more militant Frederick Douglass, Du Bois opposed Booker T. Washington's accommodational philosophy, nevertheless commending Washington's emphasis upon education as an instrument for solving racial conflict.

Du Bois sponsored a highly visible Pan-African Conference in London in 1945, advocating "rights of responsible government" for black colonies and "integrity and independence for oppressed black nations."

His belief in fostering separation of the races conflicted with the NAACP's emerging goal of

Place stamp here

integration. He was dismissed by the NAACP in 1948 for his political activity and attacks on its Executive Secretary.

Discouraged over continuing racism and society's slow efforts at reform, Du Bois moved to Ghana in 1961, became a citizen at age 93, and died two years later on the day of the Reverend Martin Luther King's historic march on Washington.

The Du Bois stamp, designed by Higgins Bond of Teaneck, New Jersey, is the 15th addition to the Postal Service's Black Heritage Series. Its first day of issue ceremony was at Atlanta, Georgia on January 31, 1992.

*W.E.B. Du Bois, with cane at right, joined marches to protest lynchings and race riots besides writing against racism. Below, Du Bois, circa 1909, in his Atlanta University office before he joined the NAACP.*

*Not long after Higgins Bond of Teaneck, NJ shifted her college studies from psychology to art she was producing praiseworthy artwork for major corporations. Designer of 1991's Jan Matzeliger stamp, Bond repeats with this year's W.E.B. Du Bois Black Heritage Series stamp.*

# Love

*Romantic Victorian art decorated pages similar to these from an 1882 book of Alfred Tennyson's poetry.*

"How do I love thee? Let me count the ways," wrote Victorian poet Elizabeth Barrett, whose heart was stirred to admiration for Robert Browning's soul and poetry even before they met.

So she counted the ways. Within the 14-line discipline of her sonnet, she described life's sublime emotion and promised, if God willed, "I shall but love thee better after death." Browning, the object of her love, never saw this or others of her "Sonnets from the Portuguese" until after their marriage.

Just as poets can "count the ways," artists can portray the sentiment, as this year's Love stamp and its predecessors since 1973 have shown. A large red heart emerging from an envelope conveys the message that love speaks in many ways, especially in personal, intimate letters, cards and valentines.

Love letters have always been part of the fabric of history, drama and art. The course of true love doesn't always run smoothly, as we know from Romeo and Juliet's tragic story. The obstacle to their love was a family feud that obsessed their parents. In Elizabeth Barrett's and Robert Browning's happier story, although a possessive father denied her a normal courtship, Britain's Penny Post, introduced in 1840, permitted the two poets to write as long and as often as they wished. And they did, taking advantage of the four-times-a-day delivery of mail to speed their letters across London.

Realizing her father would never consent to her marriage, Elizabeth eloped to France with Robert. Outraged at her temerity in leaving him, Mr. Barrett saved unopened all the letters she wrote him over the years seeking his love, understanding and forgiveness. They were given to her after his death. Although she grieved over the parental rift, Elizabeth Barrett Browning, a life-long invalid, and her loving husband lived happily until her premature death. Robert Browning never remarried.

The 1992 Love stamp was designed by veteran stamp designer Uldis Purins of Boston, Massachusetts, based on a concept offered by Richard Sheaff, a Design Coordinator for the Citizens Stamp Advisory Committee. Its first day of issue ceremony was held in Loveland, Colorado, on February 6, 1992.

*The only artist represented by two unrelated commemoratives in 1992, Uldis Purins, designer of the Love stamp, also produced the New York Stock Exchange stamp.*

# Dr.Theodore von Kármán

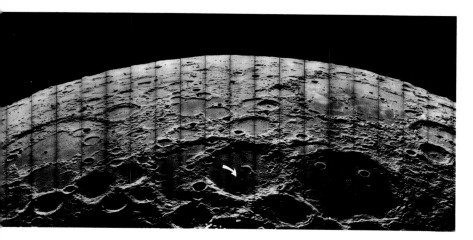

*An arrow marks the moon crater named in honor of Theodore von Kármán; at right, President John F. Kennedy awards von Kármán the first National Science Award at a White House ceremony in February 1963, as Judge Victor Alfuso, center, watches.*

Theodore von Kármán exhibited as a child the creative brilliance that led to his becoming an engineer, physicist and aerodynamicist whose work pioneered principles of supersonic flight.

Born in Hungary in 1881, von Kármán studied engineering and graduated with highest honors from the Budapest Royal Technical University in 1902. He taught before working for his doctorate at the University of Göttingen in Germany.

After seeing the first airplane flight, by a Frenchman in Paris in 1908, he returned to Göttingen to assist in dirigible research and complete his doctoral degree. His interest shifted dramatically to advanced study in the emerging field of aerodynamics.

In 1912 Dr. von Kármán became director of a new Aeronautical Institute at the University of Aachen. World War I intervened in 1914 and he served four years in the Austrian Air Force. Returning to Aachen, he taught there until 1930, when he was asked to become director of the Guggenheim Aeronautical Laboratory at the California Institute of Technology (Caltech) and the Guggenheim Airship Institute at Akron, Ohio. Although reluctant to leave Aachen, he saw Nazism emerging in Germany and accepted the offers. He never regretted his decision.

Caltech's lab attracted students of aeronautical sciences from around the world. There von Kármán founded the U.S. Institute of Aeronautical Sciences and became a consultant to the U.S. Air Corps (re-named Army Air Force in September 1947) and various industries. His research contributed to fluid mechanics, turbulence theory, mathematics in engineering, aircraft structure and wind erosion of soil. He was renowned as an expert on wind tunnels and their value to scientific research.

In 1935, he announced his theory of air resistance in bodies at supersonic speed at the Fifth Volta Congress in Italy. He later demonstrated "The von Kármán theory of Vortex Trails" to the Governor of Washington state. Learning of plans to rebuild the Tacoma Narrows suspension bridge which had been blown to earth by air currents, von Kármán advised that unless construction changes were made the new bridge would also fall. Fortunately his counsel was heeded.

He became an American citizen in 1936 and in 1938 formed a group at Caltech to study rocketry. At the same time, the Army Air Corps contracted with him to improve aircraft performance—with rocketry. In 1940, he and associate Frank J. Malina demonstrated their design for a stable, long-duration, solid-propellant rocket engine—the prototype of present long-range missiles. His jet propulsion studies led to the successful flight of the Bell X-1 plane, the first aircraft to break the sound barrier.

He founded Aerojet General, a leading manufacturer of rockets and missiles. He was named chairman of the Scientific Advisory Board for the U.S. Army Air Corps in 1944, a post he held until 1955, when he became a consultant to General Dynamics Corporation.

Von Kármán proposed an international sharing

of aeronautical sciences after World War II, patterned after the Air Corps Scientific Advisory Board. His idea was adopted and sponsored by the North American Treaty Organization (NATO). He chaired the multi-nation group that became a valuable central clearing house for specialized research.

Von Kármán received many honors before his death in Aachen in 1963. Seven years later a moon crater was given his name.

Designed by Chris Calle of Ridgefield, Connecticut, the von Kármán stamp was issued on August 31, 1992 in Washington, D.C.

*At right, von Kármán computes added rocket thrust before experimental aircraft takes off at California's March Field in 1941. Present were C.B. Millikan, Martin Summerfield, von Kármán, Frank Malina and pilot, Captain Homer A. Boushey.*

*Below, left, is Chuck Yeager's precedent-setting plane, the Bell X-1, which now hangs in the Air and Space Museum in Washington, DC.*

*Chris Calle of Ridgefield, CT, the son of distinguished artist and stamp designer Paul Calle, proves the theory that excellence can be learned and inherited. Chris, designer of the 1992 Theodore von Kármán stamp, is currently creating lithographs for future stamps on Endangered Species.*

11

News was grim for the Allied forces at the beginning of 1942. The continent of Europe was falling, country by country, to Axis might. German submarines were sinking Allied ships in the Atlantic, sometimes within sight of America's Atlantic shoreline.

Half the U.S. Navy was destroyed at Pearl Harbor. Indochina was occupied, Hong Kong and Singapore surrendered to Japan. Some of Britain's finest warships were destroyed in the Pacific and the entire Pacific Basin was vulnerable to Japanese campaigns against strategic American, Dutch and British holdings. Even Australia and New Zealand were on the endangered list.

Americans were shocked into total mobilization of people and industrial resources. After Pearl Harbor, even former isolationists saw the need for unity of purpose and effort to defeat the Axis powers.

Ten stamps illustrate key events relating to America's first full year of involvement in World War II. Designed by Bill Bond of Arlington, Virginia, and issued on August 17, 1992 in Indianapolis, Indiana, the stamps are:

### B-25s take off to raid Tokyo, April 18, 1942.
Lieutenant Colonel Jimmy Doolittle led a daring raid of 16 medium bombers launched from the aircraft carrier *Hornet* some 700 miles from Tokyo. Although the bombs they dropped had little immediate impact on the war, the bold attack lifted Americans' morale and promised future victories.

### Food and other commodities rationed, 1942.
Threatened shortages of goods critical to the war effort brought about government rationing of fuel, meat, butter, sugar, shoes, cars and tires. Americans willingly surrendered their desire for

items once taken for granted, confident that their sacrifices contributed toward victory over the hated Axis powers.

### U.S. wins Battle of the Coral Sea, May 1942.
The first historic showdown of carrier warfare took place in the Coral Sea when Japanese forces sought to seize Port Moresby. Two American carriers, the *Lexington* and *Yorktown*, intercepted the Japanese and the combatants fought a fierce aerial battle. Both sides suffered costly losses—the Americans lost the *Lexington*—but America won a strategic victory by repulsing Japan's invasion effort.

### Corregidor falls to Japanese May 6, 1942.
In Japan's invasion of the Philippines, Japanese troops bottled up American-Filipino forces on the Bataan Peninsula. Isolated, on meager rations, sick and diseased, the defenders fought bravely but with little hope of victory. On April 8, after destroying ammunition supplies, some surrendered, others retreated to the offshore island of Corregidor. Under heavy attack, they realized that unless they surrendered they would be annihilated. The Americans yielded on May 6.

### Japan invades Aleutian Islands June 1942.
The Aleutians, part of Alaska, are a chain of mountainous, volcanic islands that stretch more than 900 miles westward from the Alaskan Peninsula and separate the Bering Sea from the Pacific Ocean. Japanese forces occupied the Aleutian islands of Attu and Kiska, fulfilling the anxious predictions of Alaskan Territorial officials. The stamp shows the bombing of the U.S. naval air base at Dutch Harbor on Unalaska Island on June 3, 1942. America lost some 2500 men on the islands before the Japanese were ousted in 1943.

Clockwise *B-25 medium bomber leaves aircraft carrier* Hornet *to bomb Tokyo; U.S. soldiers open WWII second front near Oran, Algeria, November, 1942; beyond repair after Coral Sea battle, the* Lexington *was abandoned and sunk by an American destroyer; women break for lunch at Vega Aircraft plant in Burbank, California . Below,* Guadalcanal *landing August 1942 was followed by six months of fighting.*

Place stamps here

**Allies decipher secret enemy codes 1942.**
Unaware the Allies had broken their codes, a large Japanese fleet steamed to attack Midway Island. The American fleet, informed in advance of the time and place of the attack, deployed two task forces ready to do battle and defeat the Japanese. Similarly, in Great Britain, cracking Axis codes significantly aided Allied strategists' ability to prepare for attacks and conduct counterintelligence.

**Yorktown lost, U.S. wins at Midway 1942.**
With advance knowledge of Japan's plans to seize Midway Island, America's naval and air forces, though smaller than Japan's, dealt a stunning defeat to the Japanese navy after four days of heated battle. The carrier *Yorktown,* a destroyer and some 100 planes were lost but the far greater losses suffered by Japan led to its loss of domination of the seas.

**Millions of women work to aid war effort.**
Total military mobilization brought about a critical need for workers to fill the jobs men left. The movement of women into jobs traditionally held only by men tested their ability to adapt. The women were not found lacking. Before the war's end, more than 10 million American men served in uniform and six million women joined the labor force.

**Marines land on Guadalcanal, August 7, 1942.**
Ten thousand Marines landed nearly unopposed on Guadalcanal, a 92-mile-long island in the Solomon Islands where the Japanese were building an airfield. On the next two nights Japanese forces counter-attacked, and for the next six months, the Marines fought jungle heat, mud, disease, and the entrenched Japanese before the last Japanese defender was evacuated. It was Japan's first defeat on land.

**Allies land in North Africa November 1942.**
Massive British-American troop landings, known as *Operation Torch* in North Africa, took German and Italian occupying forces by surprise and the action previewed future landings in Sicily, Italy and France. Reacting quickly, Axis forces occupied Tunisia, assembled a powerful force and severely damaged Allied forces and supplies. The Allied victory at El Alamein would become the turning point in the drive to defeat the Axis powers.

*Bill Bond of Arlington, VA can truthfully say "I was there" during Nazi bombing raids on London. He has translated his experiences through vivid illustrations on the 1991 and 1992 World War II miniature sheets, two of five commemorative issues scheduled through 1995.*

# Alaska Highway

I t took a grave threat to national security in 1941 to move American and Canadian officialdom to approve the 1500-mile Alaska Highway. The Japanese were threatening U.S. bases in the Pacific. A road was needed to transport war material to Alaska and to supply a string of air fields where there was a need to ferry lend-lease aircraft to Russia. Two months later, Pearl Harbor was attacked, dramatically revealing the clear and imminent danger facing Alaska, Canada and the United States.

However, as early as 1934, Alaskan Delegates had sought air and naval bases and overland linkage between Alaskan Territory and the lower 48 states. The feasibility of these schemes was admitted by the War Department but no action was taken by Congress.

In 1938, the Army Chief of Staff in Washington said the military value of a highway was "so slight as to be negligible." Canadians concurred.

In August 1941, before the U.S. Congress, voteless Territorial Delegate Anthony J. Dimond insisted: "It [the highway] is not only economically justified, but is demanded by considerations of national defense." Finally, in October, the War Department gave the green light.

Work began at Dawson Creek, British Columbia, early in 1942.

Nine thousand soldiers (mostly black), and 13,000 civilians operated tons of earth-moving equipment over challenging terrain in frigid temperatures. Less than nine months later, the U.S. and Canadian Army Corps of Engineers completed the Alcan Highway, as it was known at the time, with a bridge over the White River in far western Yukon Territory. The cost: $20 million.

Opened to civilian use in 1948, the highway, which runs mostly through Canadian territory, reduced Alaskans' isolation, offered an alternative to ocean freight, created commercial opportunities, and revealed the beauty and vast resources of a Territory one-fifth as large as the lower contiguous United States. The highway is still the only land route to Alaska, which became the 49th State on January 3, 1959.

This stamp commemorating the Alaska Highway's 50th anniversary, was designed by Byron Birdsall of Achorage, Alaska. A joint commemorative project between the U.S. Postal Service and the Canada Post, it was issued on May 30, 1992, in Fairbanks, Alaska.

*Workers drive a Jeep on rough corduroy road early in Alaska Highway's construction. At right, the sun rises over Teslin Lake, on Highway Mile 806 in Canada's Yukon.*

*Byron Birdsall, illustrator/designer of the Alaska Highway stamp, is the first resident Alaskan to design a U.S. postage stamp. Before settling in Anchorage in 1975, Birdsall traveled, painted, exhibited and sold his popular, critically-accepted art in four continents and American Samoa.*

# Dorothy Parker

Place stamp here

Dorothy Rothschild Parker was born into a moderately wealthy family in 1893. Her only solace in her unhappy, early childhood was a voracious reading habit. Perhaps her happiest days were her teens spent at Miss Dana's School in Morristown, New Jersey where her brilliance was recognized and cultivated.

She never attended college but left home at 19 when her domineering father, whom she detested, died. She played the piano for dancing classes in New York City, published her first verse and was hired in 1916 by *Vogue* magazine at $10 a week. The next year, she moved to *Vanity Fair* magazine where she earned a reputation for panning bad plays or deflating pompous egos with a crisp sentence or sometimes one word.

Dorothy and two *Vanity Fair* colleagues, humorist Robert Benchley and editor/playwright Robert Sherwood, founded the Hotel Algonquin Round Table, alias The Vicious Circle, and met almost daily at luncheon to discuss current events, the theatre and society's pretenders. Joined by some of the most creative journalists, artists, playwrights, actors, and lyricists of the era, the members' discussions became grist for publicists' mills. Dorothy's spontaneous, rapier remarks, spoken in her soft, ladylike voice, were often quoted.

Dorothy's marriage to broker Edwin Parker ended in divorce and she retained his surname. When fired from *Vanity Fair* for her acerbic theatre reviews, Benchley and Sherwood also resigned in protest. All three became regular contributors to *The New Yorker* magazine.

Dorothy's writing career wavered between feast and famine. She wrote and published poetry, short stories, collaborated on three plays, and wrote theatrical criticism and screen plays with her second husband, Alan Campbell.

She was as often depressed as merry and she suffered low self esteem. At various times she lived in New York, Europe, Hollywood, and restored an estate in New Hope, Pennsylvania. She became a political activist, urged support for the Spanish Loyalists and inveighed against the inequality of blacks in America. Along with other writers and

*Dorothy Parker poses with her dachshund, Robinson. Below, Algonquin Round Table by Hirschfeld, clockwise, left foreground: R. Sherwood; D. Parker; R.. Benchley; A. Wolcott; H. Broun, F. P. Adams; E. Ferber, G. S. Kaufman. In background: A. Lunt and L. Fontanne, F. Crowningshield, and host F. Case. (1962)*

artists, she was charged with being a Red by the House Un-American Activities Committee. She scornfully stonewalled their accusations.

Dorothy Parker died at age 73 in New York City. Her works are as fresh, timely and quotable today as when she wrote them.

The Literary Arts Series stamp was designed by Gregg Rudd of Monroe, Connecticut and was issued in West End, New Jersey on August 22.

*Greg Rudd of Trumbull, CT, captivated in his youth by the work of artist Norman Rockwell, was determined to follow his example. Now a skilled portrait artist, he has designed the Marianne Moore, Ernest Hemingway, Francis Ouimet stamps, and the 1992 Dorothy Parker commemorative stamp.*

Stamp collectors in 1992 enjoyed the unique opportunity of comparing concepts of Columbus's first voyage by a contemporary artist with those done by several artists a century ago.

In 1893, the Post Office Department issued the first U.S. commemorative stamps, popularly known as the Columbian Exposition Issue. The 16 stamps of different denominations, each printed in a single color, were selected from large popular murals or engravings from the United States and Spain. The 6-cent stamp showed a scene from a panel appearing on bronze doors in the U.S. Capitol in Washington.

The images on the modern four-stamp block, printed in vivid colors, are intimate and representational in concept, rather than the epic and panoramic grandeur displayed on the original 16 stamps.

Arlington, Virginia, artist Richard Schlecht succeeded in distilling the 16-stamp story into four simple but dramatic views. The first portrays Columbus pleading his cause before Queen Isabella of Spain; the second shows his three ships under sail, the *nao Santa Maria*, the standard full-rigged ship of that day, and the square-rigged caravels, *Niña* and *Pinta;* the third shows crewmen eagerly sighting land; and the fourth shows apprehensive seamen and natives looking at each other for a sign of friendship or hostility. Each stamp eloquently expresses the tensions of hope, search and discovery.

Discussions during World Stamp Expo '89 in Washington, D.C., led to the United States and Italian postal administrations' decision to issue the Columbian block of four stamps jointly.

The U.S. first day ceremony for the block of four stamps was held April 24 on the island of St. Croix in the Virgin Islands—believed by many scholars to be the island Columbus first visited on his second voyage to the New World on November 14, 1493.

The four 500-lira Italian stamps feature identical artwork, except that denomination and wording appear in Italian. These stamps went on sale on April 24 in Italy and at the international stamp show, Granada '92, in Granada, Spain.

On May 22, during World Columbian Stamp Expo '92 at the Rosemont-O'Hare Exposition Center, Illinois, the U.S. Postal Service reissued the classic 16-stamp Columbian commemoratives originally issued at Chicago's Columbian Exposition in 1893. The five souvenir sheets feature the 16 stamps in the same denominations, colors and designs as their century-old predecessors. The only difference is the date: the reissue stamps read 1992.

*Richard Schlecht, veteran maritime designer of 11 Transportation Series stamps, created the block of four stamps depicting scenes from Columbus's First Voyage of Discovery in1492. Schlecht divides his time doing free-lance illustration in Arlington, VA, and painting in Italy.*

Place stamps here

*When Columbus sighted the New World's shores, he thought he found Japan. Instead, Caribbean Islands Indians welcomed him.*

Two of the five colorful, stylized and action-packed Olympic Winter Sports semi-jumbo commemorative stamps feature team competition—ice hockey and bobsledding. The other three stamps picture competitors in individual events—figure skating, speed skating and slalom skiing. They were introduced in Orlando, Florida, on January 11 in conjunction with the 1992 National Figure Skating Championships held at the Orlando Arena.

The images of breathtaking speed, skill, grace and daring, skillfully created by designer Lon Busch, of St. Louis, Missouri, recall thrilling performances of finely trained and dedicated athletes giving their supreme efforts for their country.

The XVI Olympic Winter Games held at Albertville, France, from February 8 through 23 hosted some 3,000 athletes competing on behalf of 65 countries. Senegal, West Africa, was represented for the first time in Winter Olympic Games.

Television coverage via satellite carried the Winter Games throughout the world to an estimated one billion viewers who cheered, held their collective breath, hailed medal winners and empathized with those who did not win but honored the games with their effort.

The XVI Olympic Winter Stamps and the Summer Olympic Stamps celebrating the Games at Barcelona, Spain, carry the five-ring Olympic logo that identifies the United States Postal Service as a worldwide sponsor of the Games.

The 1992 Olympic Games Stamps were issued on the 60th anniversary of the III International Olympic Games Stamps issued by the U.S. Post Office Department in 1932 at Lake Placid, New York, and Los Angeles, California.

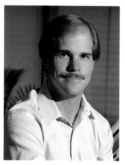

*Advertising art specialist and sports enthusiast Lon Busch of St. Louis, MO, who designed the 1991 Basketball stamp, the Pan American Games and the America/PUAS stamps, produced five stylized, colorful, action-packed Winter Olympics Sports stamps for the 1992 games in Albertville, France.*

Top center, *Speed skater Bonnie Blair won gold medals in 1988 and 1992 Winter Olympics; 500 meter speed skater, Cathy Turner won a gold medal in short track speed skating in Albertville, France; lower left, USA's four-man bobsled team in speed trials; right, USA's men's figure skating silver medalist Paul Wylie.*

Top: *USA's Eva Twardokens competed in two women's slalom events in Albertville; USA's hockey team goal-tender Ray LeBlanc in the game against Sweden at Albertville; center: Kristi Yamaguchi, U.S. figure skating gold medalist of 1992.*

*Meribel, France, the site of women's skiing and ice hockey competitions.*

Place stamps here

Place stamp here

A "stamp-on-stamp" was issued January 24, 1992, to focus on the forthcoming issuance of 20 more special commemorative stamps marking Columbus's historic voyage to the Americas.

Opening day ceremonies of the American Stamp Dealers Association's annual stamp show in Rosemont, Illinois celebrated the first day of issue of this forerunner of a series that would not only appeal to this nation but to philatelists throughout the world.

The 29-cent commemorative features a portion of the 15-cent stamp issued in 1869 from the popular "Landing of Columbus" painting by John Vanderlyn (1775-1852) in the U.S. Capitol in Washington, DC. The painting was again featured on the 2-cent stamp of the famed Columbian Series Issue of 1893. This stamp-on-stamp was designed by Richard D. Sheaff of Needham Heights, Massachusetts.

For decades, reproductions of Vanderlyn's painting appeared in elementary school textbooks. It shows Columbus pointing to the ground with his sword, symbolically taking possession of the land he discovered for Spain.
During subsequent tours of the Capitol, students were pleasantly surprised by the size of the original mural and its vibrant colors.

*Lower left:* John Vanderlyn's mural of the Landing of Columbus in the U.S. Capitol. *Above right:* Admission tickets to the 1893 World's Columbian Exposition in Chicago were masterpieces of engraving.

With the arrival of this stamp came the promise of a block of four new stamps celebrating Columbus's first voyage, issued jointly on April 24 by the United States in the Virgin Islands and the Italian postal administration in Granada, Spain.

The eagerly anticipated reissuance of the 16 Columbian Exposition Issue souvenir stamp sheets followed at the World Columbian Stamp Expo '92 in Rosemont, Illinois, on May 22-23, 1992.

*Veteran designer/typographer Richard D. Sheaff of Boston, MA designed the 1992 World Columbian Expo Landing of Columbus stamp-on-stamp. He also designed the centenary anniversary souvenir sheets of the 1893 Columbian Series, and the Columbian block of four stamps illustrated by Richard Schlecht.*

# Juan Rodríguez Cabrillo

In a commanding position on Point Loma overlooking San Diego Bay stands a statue of Juan Rodríguez Cabrillo, leader of the Spanish expedition which landed there on September 28, 1542. Their arrival marked the first time Europeans stepped ashore on the west coast of the present United States.

Point Loma's beautiful 144-acre park was dedicated in Cabrillo's honor in 1913. Although the park is said to be the most visited National Monument in the United States, relatively little is known of the man who named the area San Miguel and claimed it for Spain. No conclusive proof of his origin has been found, but many believe he was Portuguese by birth. It is unknown how he was drawn to voyages of exploration and conquest in the New World.

It is known that he arrived in Cuba in 1520 and served with Hernán Cortés in the bloody conquest of the Aztecs in Mexico. He then joined one of Cortés's officers, Pedro de Alvarado, in the invasion and subjugation of Guatemala.

When Alvarado was licensed by Spain to explore the Pacific, he chose Cabrillo to build and outfit a fleet for the task. When Alvarado died accidentally, the Spanish Viceroy ordered two explorers, Villalobos and Cabrillo, to continue explorations along the Pacific coast.

Departing from Mexico's west coast on June 27, 1542, Cabrillo pursued a northward course, stopping to replenish supplies and meet with Indians along the way. In addition to San Diego Bay, he discovered Santa Monica Bay, the Santa Lucia Mountains, and Monterey Bay; somehow he missed San Francisco Bay.

After claiming Point Loma for Spain, he continued the voyage but died of infection in a broken arm on the obscure little island he had named "Posesión" (San Miguel Island today) on January 3, 1543. On his deathbed he instructed his senior pilot to continue the explorations. Pilot Bartolomé Ferrelo probably reached the Oregon coast before returning to port.

The Cabrillo commemorative stamp, designed by Ren Wicks of Los Angeles, California, was issued on September 28, 1992, in San Diego, California.

*Their brilliant plumage mirrored on Galapagos Islands waters, flamingos search for small mollusks, crustaceans, algae and diatoms.* Facing page: *An American astronaut leaves the space shuttle "Discovery" in 1985*

*Versatile artist Ren Wicks of Los Angeles has enjoyed a distinguished career providing portraiture and illustrations for national publications and corporations. Artist/designer of the William Saroyan and William T. Piper stamps, Wicks was chosen to portray California explorer Cabrillo on a stamp.*

# Summer Olympics

Saluting the 1992 Summer Olympic Games held in Barcelona, Spain, from July 25 through August 9, the U.S. Postal Service issued a series of stamps picturing medal events considered to be among the world's most popular sports.

The stamps depicting boxing, volleyball, swimming, gymnastics, and soccer represent but 5 of the 28 official sports that brought some 15,000 entrants from five continents to Spain's sunny coast to compete in 257 medal events.

Swift, strong, agile, courageous, and disciplined young athletes, many of whom trained for a lifetime for a few minutes or even seconds of competition, proved that differences of color, religion, race, or national origin were no barriers to the highest levels of sportsmanship and excellence

Boxing and soccer had a maximum age limit: a boxer had to be under 37 to qualify, although few amateur boxers compete after 30. Many boxers who excel in the Olympic Games later become professional world champions. In soccer, called "football" outside the United States, a player could not be over 23 years old. Soccer is the most popular team sport in the Summer Olympic Games as well as the most popular game throughout the world.

High on the list of sports favored by the global audience, gymnastics feature lithe, superbly trained athletes performing feats of agility that combine skill, daring, artistry, and grace.

Volleyball, introduced as a team sport in the 1964 Olympic Games in Tokyo, appears on another Summer Olympic Games stamp. Men's and women's volleyball competition now rank as a favorite sport along with soccer and basketball.

Swimming competition, shown on the fifth Summer Olympics stamp, like another popular medal event, athletics (called track and field in the United States), almost defies limits of human strength and potential. There is always the possibility in both sports that time will be shaved from previous records.

Nearly as many journalists as there were competitors reported on the Summer Games and an estimated three billion people worldwide saw most of the games on television. The heroes and heroines were the competitors, their coaches, and their sponsors, who proved that teams from large and small nations could compete while exhibiting courage, superb athleticism, proficiency, sportsmanship, honor, and understanding to a world seeking a similar formula for peace.

The Summer Olympic Games stamps, designed by Richard Waldrep of Baltimore, Maryland, were issued in Baltimore on June 11, 1992. Each stamp bears the colorful five-ring logo of the Olympic Games, signifying that the U.S. Postal Service is an Olympic Games sponsor.

*Top Janet Evans, USA's 400 meter freestyle gold medalist in 1988 Olympic Games in Seoul, Korea; center Melissa Marlowe, USA gymnast medalist in Seoul; below USA's basketball team at the summer 1992 Tournament of the Americas; at right clockwise USA's racer Florence Griffith-Joyner won three gold medals at Seoul Olympics; Kenneth Friday, pre-Olympic boxer in 1991; Dave Johnson, decathlon entrant in 1990 Goodwill Games, competed in the 1992 Summer Olympic Games.; Karch Kiraly, of USA's gold medal volleyball team in Seoul; Cobi Jones, No. 14, of USA's soccer team in Seoul.*

*Atlanta-born Richard L. Waldrep, a partner since 1979 in Baltimore's Eucalyptus Tree Studio, illustrated the five 1992 Summer Olympics sports stamps. Nationally acclaimed and commissioned for graphics and illustration talents, he also travels widely to study butterflies in the U. S. and Neotropics.*

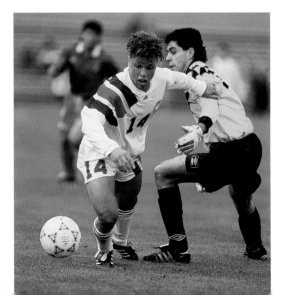

# Olympic Baseball

What will the baseball box scores look like in Arabic, Greek, Russian and South Korean newspapers wonders the American fan. To a fan they are a happy, daily ritual that describes important statistics of the previous day's or night's games.

Baseball is spreading to other countries! Although Americans may think our teams are the best, Olympic Games put that opinion to the test when other nations field their teams. Baseball became an official sport for the first time in 1992 at the Olympic Summer Games in Barcelona, Spain. It had been a demonstration sport in seven previous Games since 1912. To honor this important acceptance of one of the finest team sports, the U.S. Postal Service issued on April 3, 1992, a dramatic stamp showing a runner sliding into home plate, guarded by the opposing team's catcher, who clutches the ball in his mitt. The five-ring Olympic logo designating the U.S. Postal Service's Olympic sponsorship appears in the upper right corner of the stamp beside the 29-cent denomination.

The stamp's design, by Anthony DeLuz of Boston, Massachusetts, was chosen from 90 entries submitted in a national art contest conducted by the U.S. Postal Service.

Atlanta, Georgia, was chosen as the site to introduce the stamp because it will host the 1996 Olympic Summer Games and is the home of the Atlanta Braves, winner of the 1991 National Baseball League pennant.

*Baseball was one of the most popular events in the August 1991 Pan American Games held in Cuba.*

*Anthony De Luz, illustrator of the Olympic Baseball stamp, received a BFA degree from Eastern New Mexico State University. His career includes one-person exhibits and group shows, magazine illustrations, advertising art and courtroom artist experience.*

# Minerals

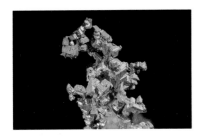

O f the four American minerals comprising the 1992 Mineral Heritage Series, the most valuable and versatile is copper, believed to be the first base metal used by man.

Earliest supplies were found in the Sinai Peninsula several thousand years ago; there were also deposits in parts of Europe and the Middle East. Now the primary copper supplying countries are the United States, Chile, Russia, Zambia, Canada and Zaire.

Copper and gold are the only metals with a distinct color other than gray in their native state. When copper is alloyed with tin, bronze results; when alloyed with zinc, brass is obtained. One can only imagine the moment several thousand years ago when early man picked up a chunk of salmon pink rock that didn't crumble when he pounded it; when he subjected it to fire, he could shape it into tools or weapons.

The copper specimen on the 1992 stamp block is from the Keewenaw Peninsula in northern Michigan, the richest and purest native deposit in this country. Native Americans were the first to use copper in that area, long before the advent of Europeans

Azurite is a beautiful blue or Prussian-blue colored mineral that has sharp transparent to translucent crystals and a brilliant glassy luster. It is found near the surface of the ground with copper deposits in Morenci and Bisbee, Arizona.

Azurite is used chiefly in jewelry, or as an ornamental display, and prized specimens can be seen in world museums.

Wulfenite, a minor ore of lead and molybdenum, is among the most beautiful minerals known. The specimen appearing on the Mineral Heritage Series was found in 1938 in Yuma, Arizona, and has become the standard by which all wulfenite finds are measured. Wulfenite is nearly opaque, and its colors can be various shades of yellow, orange, red, gray or green. It is associated with other lead ores in different localities in Austria, and New South Wales, Australia, but the United States finds in New Mexico, Nevada and Utah are the most important

The fourth mineral stamp depicts a sliced nodule of the gemstone called variscite, which is an aluminum phosphate. It is light green or emerald green in color, resembling turquoise, but is greener than turquoise and contains no copper.

Variscite's ingredients derive from the breakdown of minerals in surrounding rock. It may form veins, crystallized crusts and nodular masses. Cores of the nodules vary in color from dark green to pale green although the darker colors become paler over time, probably due to evaporation of moisture.

Variscite is cut in convex shapes and polished to create rings or necklace stones called cabochons.

The mineral stamps were designed by Len Buckley of the Bureau of Engraving and Printing and issued on September 17 in Washington, D.C.

*Photos:*
*above left, copper;*
*right, wulfenite.*

*Leonard E. Buckley, designer of the 1992 Mineral Heritage Issue, directs the Bureau of Engraving and Printing's staff responsible for developing currency, stamps, and securities designs. His previous stamp designs include the 1969 Apollo 8 and California Commemoratives, and the 1974 Mineral Heritage Issue.*

Place stamps here

# Wildflowers

With its issuance of a sheet of 50 wildflower stamps depicting diversified flowering plants native to North America and Hawaii, the U.S. Postal Service has produced a set of stamps second to none in beauty in its 145 years of philatelic history.

The Postal Service has also provided a valuable educational tool and a popular botanical identification service to the nation. No other single page of affordable art available to every person in the country has ever displayed so many native wildflowers still in existence—plants that evolved through centuries of climatic and geographic changes before early explorers and colonists entered the continent of North America.

These 50 wildflowers were not strangers to Native Americans. They found plants that had valuable medicinal properties, which they extracted and used. If plants offered food or served other useful purposes, these, too, were used. Early colonists were quick to learn about the Indians' use of remedies.

But along with human immigrants from the Old World came plant "aliens," such as dandelions, clover, chicory, mint plants, and other specimens; they found the new environment receptive and quickly took root. Many plants we consider native to this continent were imports, and most of them did not intrude upon remote parts of the nation. Those remote areas were the wildflowers' domain. Similarly, wildflowers did not prevail upon roadways and open spaces that soon became endemic to the aliens.

Unfortunately, some of our most beautiful native wildflowers are now endangered species. As the country has become more and more urbanized, and habitats once populated by wildflowers are disappearing, the ecological balance vital to the plants' existence is also disappearing. Few wildflowers can be transplanted to home gardens or botanical gardens. It has taken these plants eons to adapt to their native habitats. Without corresponding circumstances of light, soil, moisture, mineral salts, other vegetation, coexisting animal life and seasonal changes, they cannot survive.

Thousands upon thousands of Americans, young and old, have never had the joy of seeing wildflowers grow. Others who have, and who have been entranced with their beauty, dig them up and bring them home, thus contributing to the plants' extinction. It is hoped that the beauty of these stamps will encourage people to learn more about these priceless and irreplaceable wildflowers to try to save them from total annihilation.

Shortly after colonists built early settlements in this country, botanists collected specimens of native American plants and sent them to horticultural societies and collectors in England and Europe. At that time, plants were viewed more for their medicinal value than for their botanic or ornamental qualities. The wildflowers depicted on these stamps, like all plants, were given Latin names specifying the genus and species of each plant. This 18th century classification system, still in use today, avoided the confusion caused by unscientific popular names.

Many North American flowers were given popular names such as Dutchman's breeches, jack-in-the pulpit, Turk's cap lily, and lady's slipper because they resembled familiar objects. Some names, such as the Indian paintbrush, perpetuate Indian legends. The story was told that an Indian brave, after trying in vain to paint a picture of the

*Karen Mallary's art studies began in San Francisco, followed by advanced study at Spain's Prado Museum. Her expertise with flower depiction led to her selection as designer of the 50 Wildflower stamps pane. Now a Seattle resident, Mallary exhibits nationwide in galleries and juried competitions.*

sunset, asked the Great Spirit for help. The Great Spirit complied, giving the Indian paintbrushes dripping with the sunset's glorious colors, which the brave used and discarded. Wherever the brushes fell, the legend tells, plants took root and grew.

Due to the unique nature of this subject, the Postal Service has produced a collector's booklet describing the wildflowers' native habitats and some of their many uses. The booklet includes a pane of the 50 mint stamps.

The artist responsible for depicting the 50 wildflower stamps is Karen Mallary, of Seattle, Washington. They were issued on July 24, 1992, at Columbus, Ohio.

"The botanist has not been born who can complete a glossary of God's incredible inventiveness along a country road. In spring the roadsides are painted in pastels—in chartreuse, and rose, and dogwood ivory. By early summer they take on school color hues of vivid orange and blue, day lilies and lupine. After the first cutting of hay, the pastures spring up daisy-dappled, house-paint white. Beneath a parasol of Queen Anne's lace a caterpillar curls and stretches. The chicory comes and goes, flag blue, to be followed by summer asters. Actually they are not asters; they are fleabane—tiny white flowers, dime-sized eyelash fringed, with gold centers. The botanical name is Erigeron, out of the Greek for 'early old man.' That is to say, they are prematurely white. There is no controlling the honeysuckle; there is no curbing the trumpet vine. To compensate for their sprawling profusion, we get tiny things in large abundance—mayapples, buttercups, birds' foot violets, a thousand ferns as delicately fashioned as the eyelashes of a child. The trillium, loveliest of them all, kneels as modestly as a spring bride, all in white, beside the altar of an old oak stump. If you're not familiar with the trillium, imagine the flower that would come from a flute if a flute could make a flower. That is the trillium, a work of God from a theme by Mozart.

"It is a labor of love—it is more truly an act of love— to identify the wild flowers and to marvel at the purity of their grace and color. Their common names bespeak a common affection. How could Bouncing Bet be called anything else? Or Dutchman's Britches? Or Johnny Jump-Up? Or Confederate Violets? Or Basket-of-Gold?....These are the highest works of the jeweler's art, these flowers by the side of the road....All I'm saying is that the most delicate beauty, and the most perfect grace, often are found in the humblest plants along the way. There's a moral in all this, I suppose, but I pass it by."

James Jackson Kilpatrick
"The Foxes' Union" © 1977
EPM Publications, Inc.

Opposite page: *Sunflowers at San Luis Valley, Colorado;* above clockwise *Texas bluebonnets and Indian paintbrushes; shooting stars; blue flags; flowers of claret cactus; yellow lady's slipper.*

# Space

Space artists Robert T. McCall, of Paradise Valley, Arizona, and Vladimir Beilin, of Moscow, Russia, together developed a concept similar to the one Michelangelo used when he designed the ceiling of the Vatican's Sistine Chapel in Rome. God's hand reaching out to Adam's at the Creation is a metaphor for the U.S. and Russia sharing unity in space exploration in the 1992 joint issue of a block of four space stamps.

The two global powers, once highly competitive, over time have gradually shared efforts to achieve goals that would also benefit all mankind. With Earth at the bottom of the four stamps and Mars at the top, in between are depicted key space accomplishments of the former Soviet Union and the United States.

The U.S.S.R. launched the first satellite into orbit in October 4, 1957, signaling the beginning of the Space Age. In April 1961, U.S.S.R. Cosmonaut Yuri Gagarin, rocketed into space in a capsule, was the first human to make a complete orbit of Earth. Less than a month later, U.S. Astronaut Alan B. Shepard, Jr., was launched into space on top of a Redstone rocket in his capsule, Mercury 7, returned to Earth, and the race for space dominance was on! For design purposes only, the 1975 docking of U.S.A.'s Apollo and the Soviet's Soyuz is the major focus of the two lower stamps However, above the docking space ships, in the lower left stamp, appears the United States landing craft, Lunar Earth Module (LEM), as it settled on the Moon. Astronaut Neil Armstrong was the first man to step from the LEM onto the Moon's surface on July 20, 1969, six years before the Soviet and U.S. space ships rendezvoused and docked while in orbit.

Center perforations on the block of four stamps divide the Moon in half. Designs on the two upper commemoratives depict the U.S.S.R.'s manned space station and space shuttle, and the U.S. space shuttle.

Orbiting above Earth, specialists from both nations have conducted hundreds of experiments dealing with the effects of a gravity-free environment on humans and studies in medicine, astronomy, biology, materials-processing, geology and other scientific fields. Russia holds the record for a

person living the longest in a space station— approximately a year before returning to Earth.

The dominant figures on the upper stamps are a Russian Cosmonaut on the left, and an American Astronaut, on the right, in star-studded outer space reaching toward each other. Topping the block is Mars, the hoped-for destination for a three-year joint mission by Russia and the United States.

Despite the U.S.S.R.'s dissolution in 1991, Russia and the United States proceeded with the joint issue of the space commemoratives. Changes were made in the space suit logos: the former CCCP, designating the Union of Soviet Socialist Republics, was changed to GLAVKOSMOS, the name of the Russian space agency; the U.S. Astronaut's logo was changed from USA to NASA, the National Aeronautics and Space Administration. "USA" and "29" appear on this nation's stamps, "RUSSIA" on that country's stamps along with the denomination.

The postal administrations agreed to include the year of issue, 1992, on the stamps, which is customary in Russia. Precedent for this was established with the joint issue of the 1990 Sea Creature stamps.

The space exploration stamps were issued on May 29, 1992, in Des Plaines, Illinois (carrying the postmark Chicago, Illinois 60607), and in Star City, the Cosmonaut training center outside Moscow.

Place stamps here

*Facing page: American astronauts evaluate the exterior handrail system of their earth-orbiting spacecraft during a long extravehicular activity (EVA); below left, the Soviet Soyuz spacecraft as photographed from America's Apollo spacecraft before they docked in orbit over the earth; right, the Soviet crew photographed the Apollo. They joined in space for 47 hours in July 1975.*

*Veteran designers for their countries' postal administrations, Vladimir Beilin of Russia and Robert McCall, pictured above, of the United States, jointly designed and illustrated the 1992 block of four stamps featuring both nations' past space accomplishments and a hope for future shared explorations.*

# Kentucky Statehood

Place stamp here

The 200th anniversary of Kentucky's entry as the 15th state of the Union was celebrated with the issuance of a commemorative stamp in Danville, Kentucky, the site of nine constitutional conventions held between 1784 and 1792 where politicians sought separation from Virginia. On June 1, 1792, Kentucky accepted Virginia's terms for independence as a separate state of the Union and presented a constitution for its own future governance.

Virginia had claimed the land since 1776 and was loath to lose it, but the Appalachian Mountains were a difficult barrier to effective supervision. Kentucky, which entered the Union as a slave state, became a stepping-off point for settlers moving westward. Danville had the first post office in the new region.

Kentucky attracted settlers by the thousands, for whom land ownership became an obsession. However, corruption by greedy and powerful men caused many to lose their claims, among them two native sons forced to move with their families because of land-title uncertainties.

Abraham Lincoln, born in a log cabin in 1809 in Hodgenville, moved as a boy first to Indiana, then to Illinois, where he became a postmaster, lawyer, congressman, and finally was elected president of the United States. Jefferson Davis was born in 1808 in Fairview, about 100 miles from Lincoln's first home, and he too, moved, first to Louisiana, then Mississippi. He became a planter and politician, was elected to Congress and eventually became president of the Confederate States of America.

Each craved peace but the terms were rigid: union or secession. Each wanted Kentucky on his side because the state's critical location could possibly determine victory for either side. President Lincoln, after his inauguration in March 1861, said: "I hope to have God on my side, but I must have Kentucky." When Kentucky's governor issued a neutrality proclamation in May 1861, many Kentuckians moved south. In June, 9 of 10 Union candidates won elections to Congress, and Kentucky reluctantly but effectively joined the Union.

Thousands of Kentuckians fought with Union or Confederate forces, and the Reconstruction pe-

*The 1990 Kentucky Derby at Louisville's Churchill Downs; a mare and her foal sketched by artist Petro.*

*During his 40-year professional career, Kentucky native Joseph V. Petro produced acclaimed artwork ranging from scientific subjects, portraiture, fine-art paintings to sculpture. His largest project: an American medicine mural in Elizabethtown, KY. Petro regards the Kentucky Statehood stamp the "pinnacle" of his career.*

riod saw the continuation of rancor and turmoil within the state.

Several years after the war's end, Kentucky gave Jefferson Davis the land on which he was born and erected a large monument in his name. In 1880, in his last speech before his death, Davis urged reconciliation of differences and a striving toward a reunited nation.

Federal Hill, a handsome mansion near Bardstown, Kentucky, is pictured on the Statehood stamp. The home is now preserved in My Old Kentucky Home State Park as a memorial to Stephen Collins Foster, composer of "My Old Kentucky Home."

The Kentucky Statehood stamp, designed by Joseph Petro of Lexington, Kentucky, was issued at the Constitution Square State Historic Site in Danville, Kentucky on June 1, 1992.

# New York Stock Exchange

There were no traffic lights in 1870 when this lithograph of the New York Stock Exchange appeared; a century later, the floor of the NYSE still means "business."

```
┌─────────────────────────────┐
│                             │
│                             │
│      Place stamp here       │
│                             │
│                             │
└─────────────────────────────┘
```

To celebrate the 200th anniversary of the New York Stock Exchange, the U.S. Postal Service issued a stamp on May 17 that resembles a miniature stock certificate. One image shows the facade of the Stock Exchange's headquarters at 11 Wall Street; the other image portrays the famous trading floor where listed stocks affecting the financial state of the nation, individuals, and other countries are bought and sold under organized procedures.

Before the Revolutionary War, the colonies did not have their own organized exchange because most capital financing was handled in London. When the war cut off access to British capital markets, the need for investment and financing capital became crucial, leading to establishment of banks in Philadelphia and New York, issuance of Treasury bonds to refinance war debts and the 13 colonies, and the formation of a securities exchange in Philadelphia in 1790.

Two years later, 24 securities brokers, who regularly met in New York to conduct business, formulated the Buttonwood Agreement, named for the tree under which they met. The agreement established the practices of charging fixed-rate commissions and of adherence to rules of fair practice in mutual dealings.

From this modest beginning grew the organization that now plays a principal role among the world's financial institutions.

Presently more than 1,900 companies from around the world list their stocks on the New York Stock Exchange.

Serving as a model for other exchanges in the nation, the New York Stock Exchange is a corporation governed by a 21-member board of directors. Ten are elected from among principal executives of securities firms and 10 are elected from the public. The directors elect a full-time chairman who then becomes a member of the board. The Stock Exchange does not buy or sell securities or set prices. Rather, trading is conducted betweenindividual members or member groups, and the Stock Exchange provides the facilities for trading activities. Trades on the floor can only be executed by a member of the exchange. As membership is limited and a "seat" on the Stock Exchange is private property, an individual can only acquire a "seat" by sale, gift, or inheritance.

The New York Stock Exchange stamp, issued at the Federal Hall National Memorial, New York, was designed by Richard D. Sheaff of Needham Heights, Massachusetts.

Uldis Purins, designer of the New York Stock Exchange stamp, immigrated from Latvia to the United States at age 10.

Zoo specialists study, house, care for, and try to breed in captivity wild animals, whose numbers are diminishing rapidly, and whose future survival depends upon environmental regulations, ecological research, and the support of concerned people.

One center for these specialists is the National Zoological Park under the aegis of the Smithsonian Institution in Washington, D.C.

Two giant pandas, Ling-Ling and Hsing-Hsing, were gifts of the People's Republic of China to the United States in 1972, and attract the most attention of any animals in the National Zoo. Giant pandas, related to the bear family, face an uncertain future in the wild and in captivity. Technically carnivores, pandas at some point in their evolution abandoned meat as a major source of food and limited themselves to bamboo. They possess huge molar teeth and powerful chewing muscles for breaking and eating the stems, leaves and woody parts of bamboo, and their forepaws have a sixth "digit" that acts as a thumb.

Despite support from the international community, captive breeding cannot keep up with the declining numbers of pandas. It is estimated there are fewer than 1,000 giant pandas in the wild.

The other rare animal in this series of stamps is a white Bengal tiger, whose blue eyes and gray-brown stripes on whitish fur classify the beautiful cat as a mutant—a color variation of the orange Bengal tiger. All white tigers in captivity descend from a white mutant tiger captured in northern India in 1951.

A mature tiger is one of the largest cats alive and can weigh as much as 350 to 500 pounds. Its life expectancy is about 11 years.

In 1969, the tiger was listed as an endangerd species by the International Union for Conservation of Nature and Natural Resources. In 1970, Indira Gandhi spearheaded legislation banning tiger hunting in India and export of tiger skins.

Also featured in the 1992 stamp booklet are a giraffe and a flamingo, whose long necks, long legs, and gorgeous coloring appeal universally to viewers.

The giraffe is the tallest living animal and one of the four largest land animals, including the ele-

phant, rhinocerus and hippopotamus.

Although the giraffe's long neck appears to have more bones than other animals, it has seven cervical vertebrae, the same as other mammals, including man; they are just larger and more elongated.

Its legs are all the same length, although high shoulders supporting a long neck create the impression that the front legs are longer than the back. Its name derives from the Arab word *zarafa*, meaning "a creature of grace and one that walks easily."

The flamingo, whose long neck and long legs stretch out in flight to a length of 36 to 50 inches, is graceful and beautiful on land and in the air. The rosy-colored bird is closely related to the stork and, like a duck or goose, is web-footed and has a honking call. Mature flamingos are usually pink or red, the color brightest on the upper wings; their flight feathers are black, and their bills and legs are usually a bright red or yellow.

The parents take turns hatching a single egg, folding their long pink legs atop the nest. Flocks of flamingos like those once numerous in the West Indies can be seen at Florida's Hialeah Racetrack and the Bok Sanctuary.

There's no denying it, penguins are funny birds. We take great pleasure in likening them to symphony orchestra conductors, bridegrooms, and head waiters.

The king penguin, which breeds on islands off

*The giant panda, at left; opposite page, clockwise: king penguins; giraffes; flamingo; a white mutant Bengal tiger.*

*Robert Giusti, designer of the wild animal stamps, was born in Switzerland, reared in New York City, and studied art in Pennsylvania and Michigan. His expertise as art director, illustrator and designer has won him numerous prestigious awards and commissions from major U.S. and international corporations.*

Antarctica, is one of 17 different species, stands three feet tall, and is second in size only to the emperor penguin. It is easily identified by its yellow, comma-shaped ear patch that extends as a narrow line to join a golden patch on its snowy white breast. Eons ago penguins probably evolved from flying ancestors. Their wings became flippers that propel them through water to gather fish, squid, and shellfish. They have short feet with three front toes joined by a web. Their webbed feet are rudders when they swim, locomotion as they waddle, and a platform to stand on when they cover their egg.

Penguins mate for life and share nest-sitting and foodgathering for their young. Once hatched, chicks are fed predigested fish and crustaceans from their parents' mouths. When the chicks can be left alone, community baby-sitters tend them while their parents go for more food.

The five animal/bird stamps were designed by Robert Giusti of New Milford, Connecticut, and were issued on October 1 in New Orleans, Louisiana.

Place stamps here

# Christmas

Place stamp here

Collecting toys, like collecting stamps or coins, is a popular international hobby because these items are part of our history. The antique toys appearing on the block of four 1992 contemporary holiday stamps represent toys produced in the United States in the late 19th and early 20th centuries. The train and the fire engine were made of cast iron; the horse and jockey and the steamboat were made of wood.

All four were pull-toys. The wheels on the train and the fire engine were functional; the horse and jockey and the boat were mounted on platforms with wheels.

The concept of pull-toys was not original. Ancient pull-toys made of baked clay (terra cotta) have been discovered in India, in the Euphrates Valley, and in Egypt and Rhodes, dating back to 3,000 B.C., and can be viewed in museums. Some archaeologists believe toys were made for adults and were buried by early man along with food and other items intended to accompany the deceased to another world. But there is as much credibility in the theory that they were made for children.

Toys, as well as art, imitate life, and children copy their parents. So it is not farfetched to believe that a terra cotta pull-toy unearthed in Cyprus, dating from around 1,200 B.C., was as instructive and recreational for a youngster then as a train or a doll is for today's child.

Most toys were made of wood until the 19th century. Americans pioneered the production of tin toys, making small-scale models of things actually in use. Two centers of this industry were in Connecticut in the 1820s and Pennsylvania in the 1830s. Nuremburg, Germany toymakers soon played catch-up with the United States, and by 1900 Germany was exporting one-third of its toys to the United States, the rest throughout Europe.

In the mid-19th century and early 20th century, discoveries of midwestern iron deposits encouraged American toymakers to produce cast-iron toys. Most toys made before 1880 did not carry the manufacturer's mark. Many were designed for a string to be tied to the front of the toy so a child could pull it.

The traditional holiday stamp for 1992 portrays a portion of Venetian artist Giovanni Bellini's Madonna and Child with Saints, painted with oils on wood around 1490. One of some 150 works with a religious theme produced by Bellini and his studio, this painting shows a solemn Madonna looking directly at the viewer and holding her curly-haired Child before her. The painting is part of the Samuel H. Kress Collection at the National Gallery of Art in Washington, D.C.

Giovanni Bellini (c. 1430-1516), an early Renaissance artist, is considered the most important Venetian artist of the 15th century. He was named state painter of Venice in 1483, and in his later years, his most famous pupils were Titian and Giorgione.

He switched from using tempera paints to oils between 1476 and 1480 because oils were richer in color, more fusible, and more pleasing to the Venetians' sense of beauty.

German painter and engraver Albrecht Durer, famed in his own right, said of Bellini when the Venetian artist was very old, "Still he is the best painter of them all."

The contemporary stamps were designed by Louis J. Nolan of McLean, Virginia, and were issued on October 22, 1992 at Kansas City, Missouri. The traditional stamp was designed by Bradbury Thompson of Riverside, Connecticut, and was issued on October 22, 1992 at Washington, D.C.

*Madonna and Child by Giovanni Bellini, circa 1490; facing page: Strauss's Santee Clause tin wind-up, circa 1921; A.C. Gilbert's U.S. Mail tin wind-up, circa 1908; Walbert Ferry tin wind-up, 1921; Marx's wind-up Eagle Air Scout Plane, circa 1928. All toy photos courtesy of Bizarre Bazaar Ltd., New York.*

*Bradbury Thompson of Riverside, CT, one of America's most influential typographers, adds the 1992 Traditional Christmas stamp, featuring Giovanni Bellini's Madonna and Child, to the list of more than 100 stamp and stationery issues he has to his credit as a designer.*

Lou Nolan of McLean, VA demonstrates richly-deserved plaudits for his 40 years of experience as a graphic designer and illustrator with the Postal Service's 1992 block of four Contemporary Christmas stamps. Both young and old easily relate to the remembered pleasures of pull-toys.

Place stamp here

# Credits

*Dagwood's solo flight, Marx's turnover airplane windup.*

*Special acknowledgment is given to the following illustration contributors to this publication:*

**Front Cover:** © Robert Tyrrell.

**Page 2:** © National Aeronautics and Space Administration (NASA).

**Page 3:** © Art Wolfe/Allstock.

**Page 4:** Left, © David Leah/Allsport; right, © Paul Souders/Allstock.

**Page 5:** Top, Library of Congress; bottom, © Robert Tyrrell.

**Pages 6-7:** All hummingbird photos, © Robert Tyrrell.

**Page 8:** Du Bois photos courtesy of Archives of the Univesity of Massachusetts at Amherst.

**Page 9:** Two drawings, © G.W. Horland & Co.

**Page 10:** Left, courtesy Center for Earth & Planetary Studies, National Air and Space Museum, Smithsonian Institution; right, courtesy GenCorp, Aerojet.

**Page 11:** Top, courtesy Jet Propulsion Laboratory; bottom, © Ross Chapple.

**Page 12:** Far left, National Archives; center, The Bettmann Archive; top right, UPI/Bettmann Archive; center right, Library of Congress; bottom right, Bettmann Archive.

**Page 14:** Bottom left, Library of Congress; top right, © Paul Souders/Allstock.

**Page 15:** Top, Helen Iveson, Robert Iveson, Margaret Droste & Susan Cotton; bottom, © Al Hirschfeld. Drawing reproduced by special arrangement with Hirschfeld's exclusive representative, The Margo Feiden Galleries Ltd., New York.

**Pages 16-17:** © Robert Llewellyn.

**Page 18:** Top & center, © Simon Bruty/Allsport; bottom left, © Pascal Rondeau/Allsport; bottom right, © Bob Martin/Allsport.

**Page 19:** Top & bottom left, © Mike Powell/Allsport; bottom center, © Tim DeFrisco/Allsport; bottom right, © Nathan Bilow/Allsport.

**Page 20:** Bottom left, Architect of the Capitol; top right, The American Philatelist.

**Page 21:** Top, © James Randklev/Allstock; center, San Diego Historical Society Photograph Collection; bottom © Rick Stangler/Allstock.

**Page 22:** Top, © Tony Duffy/Allsport; center, © Billy Stickland/Allsport; bottom, © David Leah/Allsport.

**Page 23:** Top left, © Mike Powell/Allsport; top right, © Tim DeFrisco/ Allsport; right center, © C. Anderson/Allsport; bottom left, © Jeff Hixon/ Allsport; bottom center, © B. Hazelton/Allsport.

**Page 24:** Top & bottom left © Rick Stewart/Allsport; bottom right, © Clark Quin.

**Page 25:** Left, © Dan Behnke; right, © Chip Clark, Smithsonian Institution.

**Page 26:** Top, © David Muench/Allstock; bottom, © Steve Stroud.

**Page 27:** Top left & right,© Tom Fitzharris/Allstock; center left, © Stephen Krasemann/Allstock; center right, © John Gerlach; bottom left, © Rod Planck/ Tom Stack & Associates. Wildflower exerpt reproduced with special permission by UPS syndicated columnist, James J. Kilpatrick.

**Page 29:** All photos courtesy NASA.

**Page 30:** Top, © Churchill Downs, Inc./Kinetic Corp.; center, © Joseph Petro.

**Page 31:** Top right, © Museum of the City of New York, gift of Mrs. Beverly R. Robinson; bottom left, © Joe McNally.

**Page 32:** Top, © Art Wolfe/Allstock.

**Page 33:** Top left, © Frans Lanting/Allstock; top right, © Lew Eatherton/Allstock; right center, © Ron Sanford/Allstock; bottom, © Steve Kaufman/Allstock.

**Page 34:** Top, The National Gallery of Art, Samuel H. Kress Collection.

**Page 35:** All toy photos © David Stubbs, Bizarre Bazaar, Ltd.

**Page 36:** © Steven Mark Needham, Bizarre Bazaar, Ltd.

**Back Cover:** © Tim DeFrisco/Allsport.

*Special thanks are extended to the following individuals for their contributions to the production of this book:*

**Jeanne O'Neill,** *narrative text, research and editing.*

**Phil Jordan, Julie Schieber,** *design and art production.*

**Sara Day,** *editing and fact verification.*

**Editorial Experts, Inc.,** *editing.*

**Terrence McCaffrey,** *creative direction and print quality control.*

**Paul Ovchinnikoff,** *print production procurement and supervision.*

**Susan Robb,** *visual research.*

Front cover:
*Ruby-throated hummingbird.*

Back cover:
*Kristi Yamaguchi, USA gold medal figure skating champion.*